ANYONE WHO HAS EVER PLANTED A GARDEN knows what a pleasure it is to nurture tiny seeds and watch them grow into beautiful flowers or delicious vegetables. Whether you are an experienced gardener or just starting out, your efforts can can be immensely satisfying, and the results are sure to be a charming extension of your home.

IN GOD'S GARDEN: *A Personal Gardening Planner* is designed to help you plan your garden according to your specific needs and goals. You will learn how to prepare the soil before planting, be able to design your garden on paper before you begin digging, keep a record of your successes, and note ideas for the following year. This invaluable tool will serve as the perfect diary and resource for gardeners who are committed to a year-round hobby — as well as those who simply want a few fresh vegetables at the end of the summer.

AS YOUR SKILLS BEGIN TO IMPROVE, you'll see that gardening truly is a pleasure that grows over time . . . and a constant reminder of the wonders of God's creation.

IN GOD'S GARDEN

A PERSONAL GARDENING PLANNER

Caroline Ash

JUBILEE PUBLISHING, INC.

A DORLING KINDERSLEY BOOK

Design Bernard Higton

Managing Editor Jemima Dunne
Managing Art Editor Philip Gilderdale
Senior Art Editor Karen Ward
Project Editor Annelise Evans
Production Maryann Rogers

Special photography Guy Ryecart,
Clive Streeter, Meg Sullivan
Border illustration Jane Thomson
Stylist Suzy Gittins

This edition published in the United States by
Jubilee Publishing, Inc.
Post Office Box 30
Lebanon, TN 37088

To order, contact:
Christian Network International, Inc. (CNI)
5584 Mountain View Road
Nashville, TN 37013-2311
Phone: (800) 933-7161
FAX: (615) 641-5566

ISBN 1-57727-118-1

Color reproduction in Italy by GRB Editrice, Verona
Printed and bound by Tien Wah Press, Singapore

04 03 02 01 00 99 98
  8 7 6 5 4 3 2 1

CONTENTS

Introduction 4

INTRODUCTION

No matter what the current season, the splendor of God's creation is all around us. Whether it's the tender greens of spring, the vivid flowers of summer, the luscious fruits and bold leaves of fall, or the white sweep of winter, God has arranged a colorful palate for our pleasure.

Creating a beautiful garden is a considerable achievement, demanding both horticultural and design skills for an integrated and lovely result. So if you're a garden lover, this book is for you. It will enable you to make lists of plants you would like to grow (or grow more of), increase your knowledge of different types of gardens, and encourage you to jot down combinations that appeal to you. This diary of your garden and what happens each month will be invaluable as you create that perfectly suited to you, yet everchanging effect that you want. Gardening truly *is* a pleasure that grows over time. So don't forget to enjoy your hard work – and thank God for his colorful blessings.

GARDEN DESCRIPTION

SIZE OF GARDEN

....

TYPE OF SOIL

....

LOCAL CLIMATE

....

ASPECT

....

DESCRIPTION OF BOUNDARIES

....

STRONG FEATURES

....

WEAK FEATURES

....

AREAS FOR IMPROVEMENT

PHOTOGRAPH OF YOUR GARDEN

....

I hold that the best purpose of a
garden is to give delight and to give
refreshment of mind, to soothe, to refine,
and to lift up the heart.

GERTRUDE JEKYLL

PART ONE

CREATING YOUR GARDEN

This section will help you plan your garden,
keep detailed notes on its planting and development,
and record all your gardening activities.

FAVORITE PLANTS

When deciding on suitable plants for your garden, you are likely to begin by choosing plants that are your favorites for a variety of reasons – because they are visually appealing, because they complement the other plants, or because you feel they are essential to have in a garden. However, when choosing potential plants, it is also worth considering other factors: the flowers; the type and color of foliage; the potential height, spread, and shape of the plant; and its season of interest. Take into account the type of soil you have, and its condition, and the amount of sun or shade different parts of your garden offer. All this information will enable you to choose plants to display the beauty of God's creation for as long as possible. In the fall and winter, when few plants produce flowers, make a note of those that produce spectacular foliage, berries, or fruits.

PERENNIALS

NAME ....
SIZE AND SHAPE ....
KEY FEATURE ....
BEST SEASON ....
PLANT NEEDS ....

NAME ....
SIZE AND SHAPE ....
KEY FEATURE ....
BEST SEASON ....
PLANT NEEDS ....

NAME ....
SIZE AND SHAPE ....
KEY FEATURE ....
BEST SEASON ....
PLANT NEEDS ....

NAME ....
SIZE AND SHAPE ....
KEY FEATURE ....
BEST SEASON ....
PLANT NEEDS ....

NAME ....
SIZE AND SHAPE ....
KEY FEATURE ....
BEST SEASON ....
PLANT NEEDS ....

NAME ....
SIZE AND SHAPE ....
KEY FEATURE ....
BEST SEASON ....
PLANT NEEDS ....

NAME ....
SIZE AND SHAPE ....
KEY FEATURE ....
BEST SEASON ....
PLANT NEEDS ....

NAME ....
SIZE AND SHAPE ....
KEY FEATURE ....
BEST SEASON ....
PLANT NEEDS ....

NAME ....
SIZE AND SHAPE ....
KEY FEATURE ....
BEST SEASON ....
PLANT NEEDS ....

NAME ....
SIZE AND SHAPE ....
KEY FEATURE ....
BEST SEASON ....
PLANT NEEDS ....

NAME ....
SIZE AND SHAPE ....
KEY FEATURE ....
BEST SEASON ....
PLANT NEEDS ....

ANNUALS AND BIENNIALS

NAME
....
SIZE AND SHAPE
....
KEY FEATURE
....
BEST SEASON
....
PLANT NEEDS
....

NAME
....
SIZE AND SHAPE
....
KEY FEATURE
....
BEST SEASON
....
PLANT NEEDS
....

NAME
....
SIZE AND SHAPE
....
KEY FEATURE
....
BEST SEASON
....
PLANT NEEDS
....

NAME
....
SIZE AND SHAPE
....
KEY FEATURE
....
BEST SEASON
....
PLANT NEEDS
....

NAME
....
SIZE AND SHAPE
....
KEY FEATURE
....
BEST SEASON
....
PLANT NEEDS
....

BULBS

NAME
....
SIZE AND SHAPE
....
KEY FEATURE
....
BEST SEASON
....
PLANT NEEDS
....

NAME
....
SIZE AND SHAPE
....
KEY FEATURE
....
BEST SEASON
....
PLANT NEEDS
....

NAME
....
SIZE AND SHAPE
....
KEY FEATURE
....
BEST SEASON
....
PLANT NEEDS
....

NAME
....
SIZE AND SHAPE
....
KEY FEATURE
....
BEST SEASON
....
PLANT NEEDS
....

NAME
....
SIZE AND SHAPE
....
KEY FEATURE
....
BEST SEASON
....
PLANT NEEDS
....

NAME
....
SIZE AND SHAPE
....
KEY FEATURE
....
BEST SEASON
....
PLANT NEEDS
....

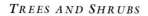

TREES AND SHRUBS

NAME ....

SIZE AND SHAPE ....

KEY FEATURE ....

BEST SEASON ....

PLANT NEEDS ....

NAME ....

SIZE AND SHAPE ....

KEY FEATURE ....

BEST SEASON ....

PLANT NEEDS ....

NAME ....

SIZE AND SHAPE ....

KEY FEATURE ....

BEST SEASON ....

PLANT NEEDS ....

NAME ....

SIZE AND SHAPE ....

KEY FEATURE ....

BEST SEASON ....

PLANT NEEDS ....

NAME ....

SIZE AND SHAPE ....

KEY FEATURE ....

BEST SEASON ....

PLANT NEEDS ....

NAME ....

SIZE AND SHAPE ....

KEY FEATURE ....

BEST SEASON ....

PLANT NEEDS ....

NAME ....

SIZE AND SHAPE ....

KEY FEATURE ....

BEST SEASON ....

PLANT NEEDS ....

NAME ....

SIZE AND SHAPE ....

KEY FEATURE ....

BEST SEASON ....

PLANT NEEDS ....

NAME ....

SIZE AND SHAPE ....

KEY FEATURE ....

BEST SEASON ....

PLANT NEEDS ....

NAME ....

SIZE AND SHAPE ....

KEY FEATURE ....

BEST SEASON ....

PLANT NEEDS ....

NAME ....

SIZE AND SHAPE ....

KEY FEATURE ....

BEST SEASON ....

PLANT NEEDS ....

NAME ....

SIZE AND SHAPE ....

KEY FEATURE ....

BEST SEASON ....

PLANT NEEDS ....

CLIMBERS

NAME
....

SIZE AND SHAPE
....

KEY FEATURE
....

BEST SEASON
....

PLANT NEEDS
....

NAME
....

SIZE AND SHAPE
....

KEY FEATURE
....

BEST SEASON
....

PLANT NEEDS
....

NAME
....

SIZE AND SHAPE
....

KEY FEATURE
....

BEST SEASON
....

PLANT NEEDS
....

NAME
....

SIZE AND SHAPE
....

KEY FEATURE
....

BEST SEASON
....

PLANT NEEDS
....

NAME
....

SIZE AND SHAPE
....

KEY FEATURE
....

BEST SEASON
....

PLANT NEEDS
....

NAME
....

SIZE AND SHAPE
....

KEY FEATURE
....

BEST SEASON
....

PLANT NEEDS
....

NAME
....

SIZE AND SHAPE
....

KEY FEATURE
....

BEST SEASON
....

PLANT NEEDS
....

The heavens belong to
the LORD, but he has given
the earth to all humanity.
PSALM 115:16 NLT

NAME
....

SIZE AND SHAPE
....

KEY FEATURE
....

BEST SEASON
....

PLANT NEEDS
....

NAME
....

SIZE AND SHAPE
....

KEY FEATURE
....

BEST SEASON
....

PLANT NEEDS
....

NAME
....

SIZE AND SHAPE
....

KEY FEATURE
....

BEST SEASON
....

PLANT NEEDS
....

NAME
....

SIZE AND SHAPE
....

KEY FEATURE
....

BEST SEASON
....

PLANT NEEDS
....

NAME
....

SIZE AND SHAPE
....

KEY FEATURE
....

BEST SEASON
....

PLANT NEEDS
....

GARDEN PLANS

These grids can be used to draw a scaled-down plan of your garden and record the position of existing plants, or to plan future planting areas. Plants may be numbered on each grid and the plant names entered beside the corresponding number in the key accompanying the grid. No garden ever remains the same for any length of time, and you will probably want to alter these plans to incorporate new planting, and changes to your garden, as it develops and matures. Alternatively, photocopy these pages so that you can refine your plans as your garden changes over the years.

KEY TO AREA ONE

1
2
3
4
5
6
7

8
9
10
11
12
13
14
15
16

17
18
19

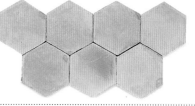

20
21
22
23
24
25
26
27
28
29
30

The one who sows to please the Spirit,
from the Spirit will reap eternal life.
GALATIANS 6:8 NIV

AREA ONE

AREA TWO

KEY TO AREA TWO

1
2
3
4
5
6
7
8
9
10
11
12

Dear King of forest glades and garden,
O God, I adore Thee;
I'll take root where I am planted,
Content to bring Thee glory.

JILL BRISCOE, *KING OF GLORY*

13
14
15
16
17
18
19
20
21
22

AREA THREE

KEY TO AREA THREE

1
2
3
4
5
6
7
8

9
10
11
12
13
14
15
16

17
18
19
20
21
22
23
24

PLANTING RECORDS

Keeping a record of any new plants you acquire is extremely useful. If you wish to purchase a similar plant in the future, you can use these notes to look up the name and description of the plant and the supplier. This record also serves as a reminder in years to come, when the plant label has faded or disappeared from the garden. Planting a tree or long-lived shrub or climber not only gives a structure to your garden, but is an investment in caring for God's good earth – as God instructed Adam and Eve to do in Genesis. Your records may also intrigue future owners of your garden.

PERENNIALS

NAME	WHERE PURCHASED	WHERE PLANTED	DATE

ANNUALS AND BIENNIALS

NAME	WHERE PURCHASED	WHERE PLANTED	DATE

BULBS

NAME	WHERE PURCHASED	WHERE PLANTED	DATE

SHRUBS

NAME	WHERE PURCHASED	WHERE PLANTED	DATE

Faith is a living thing, a plant that needs constant feeding on a daily basis.

DAVID WATSON, *FEAR NO EVIL*

CLIMBERS

NAME	WHERE PURCHASED	WHERE PLANTED	DATE

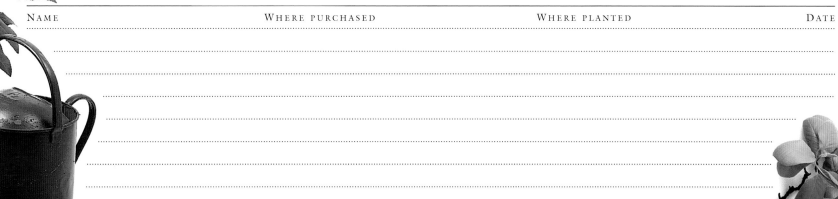

TREES

NAME	WHERE PURCHASED	WHERE PLANTED	DATE

PROPAGATION

Increasing your stock of plants by propagation is both economical and rewarding as long as you follow the basic guidelines and choose a suitable technique. There are four principal methods: you can raise plants from seed, or from cuttings; or through division; or layering. Growing plants from seed is very satisfying, although some seed is difficult or slow to germinate. It is the easiest method of raising a large number of plants, and is the best means of propagation for many herbaceous plants. Taking cuttings is the most widespread vegetative practice, although it does demand a degree of skill. Once mastered, it is a reliable means of propagating a plant with the same characteristics as its parent. Division is the simplest method, and many clump-forming perennials and bulbs benefit from dividing. Layering is commonly used for trees, shrubs, and climbers, as growing these plants from seed can be an extremely slow process.

RECORD OF SEEDS SOWN

NAME	DATE SOWN	DATE GERMINATED	DATE TRANSPLANTED	COMMENTS

In seed time learn, in harvest teach, in winter enjoy.
WILLIAM BLAKE, *THE MARRIAGE OF HEAVEN AND HELL*

RECORD OF CUTTINGS

PARENT PLANT	DATE TAKEN	DATE ROOTED	COMMENTS

RECORD OF DIVISION

PARENT PLANT	DATE DIVIDED	DATE PLANTED OUT	COMMENTS

RECORD OF LAYERING

PARENT PLANT	DATE TAKEN	DATE LAYERED	COMMENTS

VEGETABLES

Cultivating your own food satisfies a basic instinct, and has many advantages. Little can match the flavor of freshly picked, home-grown vegetables, and varieties that are unusual or difficult to obtain can be grown in abundance and without the use of chemicals. Growing your own food also saves money. A gardener can feel proud of being able to feed his friends and family with produce harvested from the garden. If space is at a premium, vegetables can be grown successfully in a wide variety of containers or can be incorporated in a mixed border. Many can be grown vertically, instead of only at ground level, and will grow happily up tepees of stakes or other frames. Choose compact and fast-growing varieties and plant a small amount of each crop. By successive planting of seasonal crops it is possible to maximize the harvest reaped in a confined space.

RECORD OF VEGETABLES GROWN

NAME

DATE PLANTED   DATE HARVESTED

COMMENTS ON CROP

NAME

DATE PLANTED   DATE HARVESTED

COMMENTS ON CROP

NAME

DATE PLANTED   DATE HARVESTED

COMMENTS ON CROP

NAME

DATE PLANTED   DATE HARVESTED

COMMENTS ON CROP

NAME

DATE PLANTED   DATE HARVESTED

COMMENTS ON CROP

NAME

DATE PLANTED   DATE HARVESTED

COMMENTS ON CROP

Then God said, "Let the land produce vegetation." And it was so.
GENESIS 1:11 NIV

NAME ....

DATE PLANTED .... DATE HARVESTED ....

COMMENTS ON CROP ....

NAME ....

DATE PLANTED .... DATE HARVESTED ....

COMMENTS ON CROP ....

NAME ....

DATE PLANTED .... DATE HARVESTED ....

COMMENTS ON CROP ....

NAME ....

DATE PLANTED .... DATE HARVESTED ....

COMMENTS ON CROP ....

CHECKLIST OF TASKS

Spring
Plant out perennial vegetables; start planting out annual vegetables, under cover if necessary; mulch in late spring; water thoroughly; sow seed of tender vegetables indoors, and seed of hardy vegetables outdoors.

Summer
Plant out winter brassicas, salad vegetables and tender vegetables; water as necessary; train climbing vegetables; harvest and store produce; sow seed of summer crops; begin sowing seed of winter vegetables.

Fall
Plant out winter salad vegetables under cover; start preparing empty beds; harvest and store produce; protect tender crops and perennials; sow seed of salad crops under cover.

Winter
Finish preparing empty beds; prepare seedbeds; stake and protect vegetables as necessary; sow seed indoors.

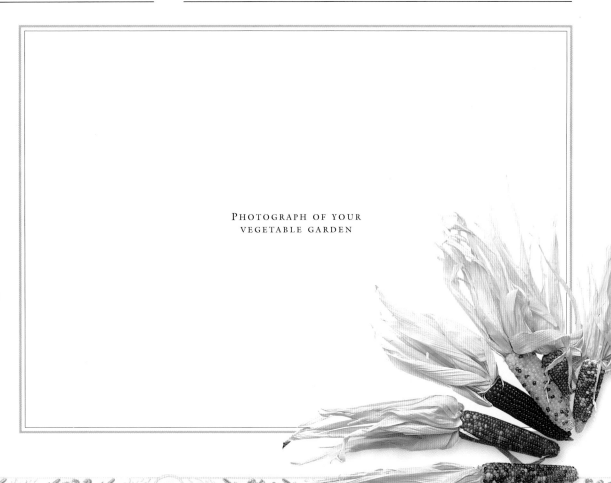

PHOTOGRAPH OF YOUR
VEGETABLE GARDEN

FRUIT

While growing vegetables frequently requires intensive labor, fruit trees and bushes usually need less attention. However, many fruit trees require pruning, thinning, and spraying, and bushes need to be tied in. If possible, choose disease-resistant, long-lived varieties. A fruit tree can form a focal point among herbaceous perennials, contributing glorious blossoms in the spring, and colorful foliage and fruits later in the year. Fruit bushes can be planted in a mixed border, as long as there is easy access for picking. Many dwarf varieties of fruit trees have been bred to grow and flourish in containers.

RECORD OF FRUIT TREES GROWN

NAME

DATE PLANTED   DATE HARVESTED

COMMENTS ON CROP

NAME

DATE PLANTED   DATE HARVESTED

COMMENTS ON CROP

NAME

DATE PLANTED   DATE HARVESTED

COMMENTS ON CROP

NAME

DATE PLANTED

DATE HARVESTED

COMMENTS ON CROP

NAME

DATE PLANTED   DATE HARVESTED

COMMENTS ON CROP

NAME

DATE PLANTED   DATE HARVESTED

COMMENTS ON CROP

NAME

DATE PLANTED   DATE HARVESTED

COMMENTS ON CROP

NAME

DATE PLANTED

DATE HARVESTED

COMMENTS ON CROP

PLANTS NEEDING SPECIAL ATTENTION

NAME
_____

SPECIAL NEEDS
_____

NAME
_____

SPECIAL NEEDS
_____

NAME
_____

SPECIAL NEEDS
_____

CHECKLIST OF TASKS

Spring
Begin to feed, mulch, and water fruits; check nets, stakes, and ties; pollinate as necessary; prune stone-fruit trees and trained trees; bark-ring apple and pear trees as necessary.

Summer
Replenish mulch and give liquid feed; water as required; thin out tree fruits if needed; pinch out and train shoots of fan-trained trees; prune summer-fruiting raspberries; summer-prune trained apples, pears, and plums; take leaf-bud cuttings of blackberries.

Fall
Plant tree, bush, and cane fruits; transplant fruit trees; harvest fruits, burn debris and store produce; check stakes and ties; remove old canes and tie in new ones; plant runners and sow seed of strawberries; winter-prune apples, pears, and fruit bushes; divide rooted suckers of raspberries.

Winter
Plant tree, bush, and cane fruits; protect tender outdoor fruits; repot or top-dress container-grown fruits; prune blackcurrants and blackberries.

A ll things bright and beautiful, all creatures great and small, All things wise and wonderful, the Lord God made them all. The cold wind in the winter, the pleasant summer sun, The ripe fruits in the garden, He made them every one.

MRS C. F. ALEXANDER,
*ALL THINGS BRIGHT
AND BEAUTIFUL*

RECORD OF SOFT FRUIT GROWN

NAME
_____

DATE PLANTED   DATE HARVESTED
_____

COMMENTS ON CROP
_____

NAME
_____

DATE PLANTED   DATE HARVESTED
_____

COMMENTS ON CROP
_____

NAME
_____

DATE PLANTED   DATE HARVESTED
_____

COMMENTS ON CROP
_____

NAME
_____

DATE PLANTED   DATE HARVESTED
_____

COMMENTS ON CROP
_____

NAME
_____

DATE PLANTED   DATE HARVESTED
_____

COMMENTS ON CROP
_____

NAME
_____

DATE PLANTED   DATE HARVESTED
_____

COMMENTS ON CROP
_____

THE HERB GARDEN

Herbs need to be readily accessible if they are to be picked and used, so it is best to position them near the kitchen door. They can be grown among other plants, in pots, or in a herb garden. Many herbs originate from the Mediterranean; these flourish in poor soil in a bright, sunny spot. Growing your own guarantees an abundant supply. Gather fresh herbs at their peak and use them immediately, or dry them for use throughout the year. Frequent cutting and trimming of herbs prompts new growth and means you can pick your herbs as you need them. Most herbs require little maintenance, apart from an annual cut-back and trimming. Foliage removed when pruning can be used in the kitchen as needed. Herbs are valued for many reasons, and are grown not only for their culinary uses, but for medicinal and cosmetic purposes.

RECORD OF HERBS GROWN

NAME	DATE PLANTED
USES	

NAME	DATE PLANTED
USES	

NAME	DATE PLANTED
USES	

NAME	DATE PLANTED
USES	

NAME	DATE PLANTED
USES	

NAME	DATE PLANTED
USES	

NAME	DATE PLANTED
USES	

NAME	DATE PLANTED
USES	

NAME	DATE PLANTED
USES	

NAME	DATE PLANTED
USES	

NAME	DATE PLANTED
USES	

Speak not – whisper not;
Here bloweth thyme and bergamot;
Softly on the evening hour,
Secret herbs their spices shower.

WALTER DE LA MARE,
THE SUNKEN GARDEN

ROCK PLANTS

Rock-garden plants originate in alpine conditions and thrive on what appears to be inhospitable terrain, on rocky, thin soils. Well-drained rock or gravel gardens provide ideal conditions, as most rock-garden plants grow best in an open, sunny place, although some prefer the shade provided by rocks. Many are ideal for growing in cracks and crevices. The majority of rock-garden plants are small and compact to reduce their wind resistance, and are able to withstand extreme weather conditions, from heavy snow to brilliant sunshine. Their compact growing habit and tough, leathery, or hairy leaves help conserve moisture, making them drought-tolerant. The key to success with rock-garden plants is to keep them from becoming too wet in winter, as they will rot. Once established, most plants require minimal maintenance and will continue to flower happily for years.

RECORD OF ROCK GARDEN PLANTS GROWN

NAME

WHEN IN FLOWER   DATE PLANTED

NAME

WHEN IN FLOWER   DATE PLANTED

NAME

WHEN IN FLOWER   DATE PLANTED

NAME

WHEN IN FLOWER   DATE PLANTED

NAME

WHEN IN FLOWER   DATE PLANTED

NAME

WHEN IN FLOWER   DATE PLANTED

NAME

WHEN IN FLOWER   DATE PLANTED

NAME

WHEN IN FLOWER   DATE PLANTED

NAME

WHEN IN FLOWER   DATE PLANTED

NAME

WHEN IN FLOWER   DATE PLANTED

NAME

WHEN IN FLOWER   DATE PLANTED

NAME

WHEN IN FLOWER   DATE PLANTED

Trust in the LORD forever, for the LORD,
the LORD, is the Rock eternal.

ISAIAH 26:4 NIV

CONTAINERS

Almost any container looks attractive in the garden; old stone sinks and wooden barrels are classic favorites. Terra-cotta or glazed pots are readily available, while copper, lead, and stone containers add a unique touch. Containers are also useful for growing plants that can be used to fill in gaps in borders. The only requirements are that the container must have drainage holes in the bottom and should be able to withstand wind, rain, and frost. Some pots do not even need the addition of plants to look beautiful – think of them as pieces of sculpture.

Plain pots can provide a peaceful contrast to colorful planting; by the same token, brightly colored containers will enliven a quiet corner of the garden. Window boxes and hanging baskets are an attractive way to grow plants at different heights, rather than restricting everything to ground level.

POTS

DESCRIPTION

DATE PLANTED

SEASON OF INTEREST

PLANTS

DESCRIPTION

DATE PLANTED

SEASON OF INTEREST

PLANTS

DESCRIPTION

DATE PLANTED

SEASON OF INTEREST

PLANTS

DESCRIPTION

DATE PLANTED

SEASON OF INTEREST

PLANTS

HANGING BASKETS

DESCRIPTION

DATE PLANTED

SEASON OF
INTEREST

PLANTS

DESCRIPTION

DATE PLANTED

SEASON OF INTEREST

PLANTS

DESCRIPTION

DATE PLANTED

SEASON OF INTEREST

PLANTS

DESCRIPTION

DATE PLANTED

SEASON OF INTEREST

PLANTS

WINDOW BOXES

DESCRIPTION

DATE PLANTED

SEASON OF INTEREST

PLANTS

DESCRIPTION

DATE PLANTED

SEASON OF INTEREST

PLANTS

DESCRIPTION

DATE PLANTED

SEASON OF INTEREST

PLANTS

DESCRIPTION

DATE PLANTED

SEASON OF INTEREST

PLANTS

THE WATER GARDEN

Water adds a new dimension to the garden. Flowing water, such as a garden stream or a fountain, makes a soothing, refreshing, repetitive sound, while still water is tranquil and calming. Water draws the eye, accentuates the shape of plants by adding reflections, and gives off shimmering patterns of light. The lush green foliage of many moisture-loving plants grown around the side of a pond contrasts with those in drier parts of the garden and increases the range of plants that can be grown.

Oxygenating plants help keep the pond water clear and enable you to create your own micro-ecoclimate. Water and plants work together to create an environment attractive to wildlife. If you keep a few fish, they will keep the mosquito population down and fill the pond with color and movement.

RECORD OF WATER-GARDEN PLANTS

NAME	DATE PLANTED
DEPTH PLANTED	WHEN IN FLOWER
COMMENTS	

NAME	DATE PLANTED
DEPTH PLANTED	WHEN IN FLOWER
COMMENTS	

NAME	DATE PLANTED
DEPTH PLANTED	WHEN IN FLOWER
COMMENTS	

NAME	DATE PLANTED
DEPTH PLANTED	WHEN IN FLOWER
COMMENTS	

NAME	DATE PLANTED
DEPTH PLANTED	WHEN IN FLOWER
COMMENTS	

NAME	DATE PLANTED
DEPTH PLANTED	WHEN IN FLOWER
COMMENTS	

NAME	DATE PLANTED
DEPTH PLANTED	WHEN IN FLOWER
COMMENTS	

NAME	DATE PLANTED
DEPTH PLANTED	WHEN IN FLOWER
COMMENTS	

NAME

DATE PLANTED

DEPTH PLANTED

WHEN IN FLOWER

COMMENTS

NAME

DATE PLANTED

DEPTH PLANTED

WHEN IN FLOWER

COMMENTS

CHECKLIST OF POND TASKS

Spring
Thin out oxygenating plants; remove algae; divide and replant congested plants; carry out new planting; begin feeding fish.

Summer
Remove algae; thin out excessive growth; feed water lilies; feed fish; replenish water lost by evaporation; weed bog garden; take softwood cuttings; collect and sow seed.

Fall
Thin out underwater plants; remove dying growth and debris; net pond to keep out leaves; protect tender plants against cold; stop feeding fish.

Winter
Overhaul pump; ensure small area of surface remains unfrozen by using a heater or a floating ball or log.

DIARY OF POND LIFE

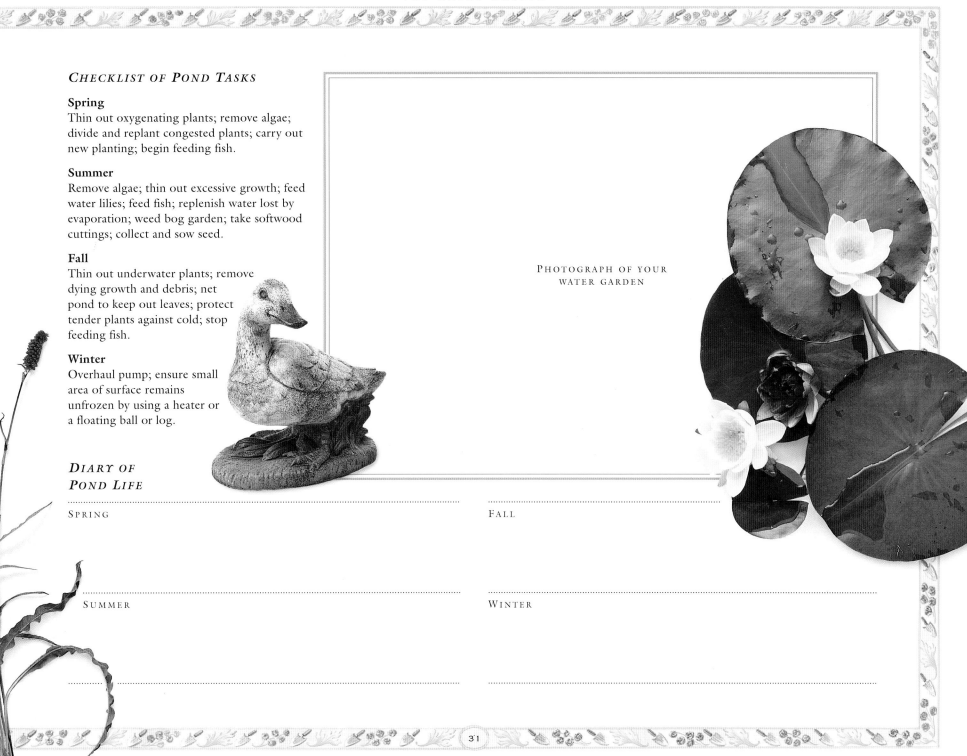

PHOTOGRAPH OF YOUR
WATER GARDEN

SPRING

FALL

SUMMER

WINTER

PART TWO

GARDEN DIARY

Use this section to make monthly notes of what happens in your garden throughout the year, and to record visits to gardens, horticultural shows, and lectures. Detailed checklists will help remind you of seasonal tasks to be undertaken.

SPRING

Spring heralds the end of winter and new growth in the garden. The first shoots of bulbs and perennials begin to emerge and leaf buds unfurl on deciduous shrubs. As the earth warms, spring bulbs come into flower. The fresh delicate green of their foliage contrasts beautifully with the cheerful hue of their blooms. Pretty pink and white blossoms add a froth of massed color. The air is clear, and the sunshine has a special brightness seen at no other time of the year. Now is the time to start sowing seed, undertake new plantings, and get ahead on routine maintenance to ensure your garden will look its best in the coming year and in the years to come.

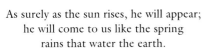

As surely as the sun rises, he will appear;
he will come to us like the spring
rains that water the earth.

HOSEA 6:3 NIV

SPRING GARDEN TASKS

Pruning
Prune deciduous shrubs and climbers
that flower on new wood, late summer-
flowering trees, and shrubby herbs.

Weeding
Control all weeds.

Mulching
Feed and mulch all established plants,
beds, and borders once the soil has
warmed up but is still moist.

Spraying
Begin spraying roses, and perennials if
necessary, against pests and diseases.

Planting
Plant out trees, shrubs, biennials, pot-
grown roses, herbs, and hardy annuals;
water new plantings frequently.

Deadheading
Deadhead bulbs and early-
flowering plants regularly unless
their seed is needed.

Sowing
Sow seeds of hardy
perennials and annuals
outdoors.

Lawns
Repair damaged areas;
sow seed or lay new turf;
Begin mowing when grass
begins to grow.

PHOTOGRAPH OF YOUR GARDEN
IN SPRING

Top-dress
Repot or top-dress all plants
in containers outdoors and
under glass.

General
Prepare greenhouse beds;
repair any winter damage to
sheds, fences, and paths; clean
paths; clean and oil or paint
garden furniture.

EARLY SPRING

TASKS TO BE DONE

*CHECKLIST OF
EARLY SPRING TASKS*

Clean up winter debris

Plant out hardy
perennials and summer-
flowering bulbs

Check tree ties and stakes

Layer trees, shrubs, and
climbers

Sow seeds of annuals
under cover

SPECIAL PROJECTS

PLANTS THAT REQUIRE SPECIAL ATTENTION

IDEAS FOR FUTURE PLANTING

Mighty God! Creator unbegun, unending! Your works
dazzle me to silence and to awe and aweful prayer.
WALTER WANGERIN, *RAGMAN AND OTHER CRIES OF FAITH*

THE GARDEN IN EARLY SPRING

PLANTS IN FLOWER

OUTSTANDING PLANTS

SUCCESSFUL COLOR SCHEMES

VERSATILE BULBS

Spring-blooming bulbs provide some of the earliest flowers of the year. Once established, they will increase annually and, with good care, will produce a profusion of flowers for many years. Bulbs extend the flowering season of planting designs before many deciduous shrubs and perennials have emerged from winter hibernation. The wide variety available means that with careful choice you can select bulbs that are suitable for any site and guarantee continuous flowers throughout the year.

After bulbs have finished flowering, remove the blooms, but allow the leaves to die down naturally so that the bulb can build food reserves for the following year. Feed with manure to promote growth for the next flowering season.

WEATHER CONDITIONS

The LORD will open the heavens, the storehouse of his bounty, to send rain on your land in season and to bless all the work of your hands.

DEUTERONOMY 28:12 NIV

MID-SPRING

TASKS TO BE DONE

*CHECKLIST OF
MID-SPRING TASKS*

Plant climbers

Introduce biological pest
controls into greenhouse

Remove suckers from
trees and shrubs

Prune and renovate
evergreen shrubs

Reseed or resod worn
areas of lawn

Pinch and/or stake
herbaceous plants

SPECIAL PROJECTS

PLANTS THAT REQUIRE SPECIAL ATTENTION

IDEAS FOR FUTURE PLANTING

The flowers are springing up, and the time of
singing birds has come. Yes, spring is here!
SONG OF SONGS 2:12-13 NLT

THE GARDEN IN MID-SPRING

PLANTS IN FLOWER

OUTSTANDING PLANTS

SUCCESSFUL COLOR SCHEMES

THE REWARDS OF PRUNING

Pruning is an important way to obtain the optimum performance from a plant, and to encourage it to produce more flowers, fruit, or foliage. It may be done to direct the growth of a young plant into a strong and attractive structure, to train a plant into a particular shape, or to keep a very vigorous plant under control. Weak, diseased, or tired shoots can be removed and the production of flowers and fruit increased. Taking out some old stems also allows light and air into a plant.

The type and time of pruning will depend on the plant – some need little attention, while others grow best when cut back hard. Plants should be fed generously after being cut back, since pruning stimulates new growth.

WEATHER CONDITIONS

LATE SPRING

TASKS TO BE DONE

SPECIAL PROJECTS

CHECKLIST OF
LATE SPRING TASKS

Prune early-flowering
shrubs

Start planting out
annuals

Sow biennials
in nursery bed or
under cover

Begin to lift and store
spring-flowering bulbs

Rake lawn and apply
fertilizer

PLANTS THAT REQUIRE SPECIAL ATTENTION

IDEAS FOR FUTURE PLANTING

The world is charged with the grandeur of God.
It will flame out, like shining from shook foil.
GERARD MANLEY HOPKINS, *GOD'S GRANDEUR*

THE GARDEN IN LATE SPRING

PLANTS IN FLOWER

OUTSTANDING PLANTS

SUCCESSFUL COLOR SCHEMES

THE BENEFITS OF MULCHING

Spring is an ideal time to apply a mulch, because the ground has begun to warm up but remains moist, and weeds have begun to proliferate. A mulch is usually a thick layer of organic matter spread on the soil surface; effective mulches include garden or used mushroom compost, well-rotted manure, shredded hardwood, straw, ground bark, or cocoa shells. Materials such as black plastic or gravel can also be used.

A mulch has a number of advantages: it conserves moisture by reducing evaporation, maintains the ground at an even temperature, keeps plant roots cool, and suppresses weeds. Organic mulches also provide nourishment for plants and improve the water retention, structure, and fertility of the soil. Some organic mulches greatly improve the appearance of a garden, as soil showing between plants can appear thin and bare.

WEATHER CONDITIONS

As long as the earth remains, there will be springtime and harvest, cold and heat, winter and summer, day and night.

GENESIS 8:22 NLT

SUMMER

With the intensive work of spring completed, the gardener can begin to slow down and enjoy watching the garden unfold, reaching a full crescendo as summer progresses. The lush summer garden boasts a profusion of flowers and a wealth of rich colors and scents, as the long, hot, days provide optimum conditions for many plants. Routine tasks such as deadheading, spraying, and staking, still need to be carried out regularly so that the carefully planned luxuriance does not become an unruly mess. Summer is ideal for entertaining in the garden, and the gardener should be able to find time to enjoy sharing the fruits of all the labors of spring with friends and family and appreciating the wonder and beauty of God's garden.

SUMMER GARDEN TASKS

Pruning
After flowering, prune shrubs and climbers that flower on old wood.

Weeding
Control all weeds.

Staking
Stake late-flowering plants that will need support; check plant ties.

Spraying
Spray plants that are prone to infestation or disease, if desired.

Deadheading
Remove faded flowers regularly unless their seed is needed.

Lawns
Mow frequently, except in dry periods.

Watering
Water containers daily
in dry weather; water newly planted and budding plants thoroughly.

Cutting back
Cut back early-flowering perennials to promote a second flush of growth.

Sowing
Collect and sow seed of early-flowering herbaceous plants and bulbs.

PHOTOGRAPH OF YOUR GARDEN
IN SUMMER

Love all God's creation.
Love every leaf,
every ray of God's light.
FYODOR DOSTOYEVSKY,
THE BROTHERS KARAMAZOV

EARLY SUMMER

TASKS TO BE DONE

CHECKLIST OF EARLY SUMMER TASKS

Shade and ventilate greenhouse

Lift and store spring-flowering bulbs

Prune spring-flowering deciduous trees and shrubs

Take softwood cuttings of climbers

Finish planting out annuals

SPECIAL PROJECTS

PLANTS THAT REQUIRE SPECIAL ATTENTION

IDEAS FOR FUTURE PLANTING

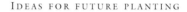

Open your eyes, my friend, and fill all your life
with the brightness of the splendor of God!
Live all your life seeing your powerful,
loving Lord at work everywhere.

ANNE ORTLUND,
THE DISCIPLINES OF THE HEART

THE GARDEN IN EARLY SUMMER

PLANTS IN FLOWER

OUTSTANDING PLANTS

SUCCESSFUL COLOR SCHEMES

STAKING

When fully grown, many modern herbaceous plants collapse under the weight of large, heavy blooms, or their slender stems may be beaten down or broken by wind and rain. Once a plant has flopped over, it is difficult to stake effectively without the supports looking unnatural and obtrusive.

It is best to stake tall or fragile plants early in the growing season – usually spring or early summer – when the foliage is still emerging. This will allow the shoots to grow through the supports into a natural form and new foliage will conceal the staking. Use individual stakes for plants with thick or single stems, and a circle of stakes and twine, or metal link stakes, for clump-forming plants. As the plants grow, remember to tie in plants at intervals to the single stakes or to raise the circular supports slightly.

WEATHER CONDITIONS

MIDSUMMER

TASKS TO BE DONE

SPECIAL PROJECTS

CHECKLIST OF
MIDSUMMER TASKS

Feed roses after
flowering

Begin to plan
fall planting

Prepare soil for
fall planting

Plant fall-flowering
bulbs

PLANTS THAT REQUIRE SPECIAL ATTENTION

IDEAS FOR FUTURE PLANTING

Plant out seedlings
of perennials
and biennials into
nursery bed

I will sing a new song
unto the Lord.
His glory has not worthily
been spoken
Though every leafy tree
and blade of grass
Whispers in the wind to tell
his hidden Name.

CHAD WALSH, *THE PSALM OF CHRIST*

THE GARDEN IN MIDSUMMER

PLANTS IN FLOWER

SUCCESSFUL COLOR SCHEMES

OUTSTANDING PLANTS

WEATHER CONDITIONS

THE VALUE OF WATER

Water is essential to plants and is especially important during the growing season. Prioritize your watering – in a dry spell, newly planted or young plants can rapidly become dehydrated, while larger, more mature plants have established root systems to search for water. Hanging baskets and containers may need watering twice a day in warm weather. Weed thoroughly so that these unwanted plants do not compete for valuable water.

Frequent light watering will evaporate quickly, encourage unwanted root growth near the dry surface, and weaken the plant, so it is best to give a garden plant or border a good, long soaking once a week. Water in the early evening, when the soil can absorb the moisture before it evaporates in the summer sun.

SUMMER BEDDING RECORD

Annuals and tender perennials used as summer bedding plants grow quickly, and provide profuse amounts of colorful flowers for a long period. They are invaluable for brightening areas of the garden that may become drab once spring bulbs and plantings have died down, or where a plant has suddenly died and left a gap. Bedding plants can also be used to fill in spaces while perennial plants are maturing and can be planted in containers for instant color.

They are commonly massed in summer beds for maximum impact, but can add a pleasing random dimension to a mixed border, particularly if they are allowed to self-seed. They offer vibrant color and delightful informality if interspersed throughout the permanent planting of a border – a technique that is especially succesful when much of the garden is not in flower. Annuals, in particular, can add a touch of tropical luxuriance.

BEDDING PLANT	SUPPLIER OR SOURCE	WHERE PLANTED	FLOWERING PERIOD

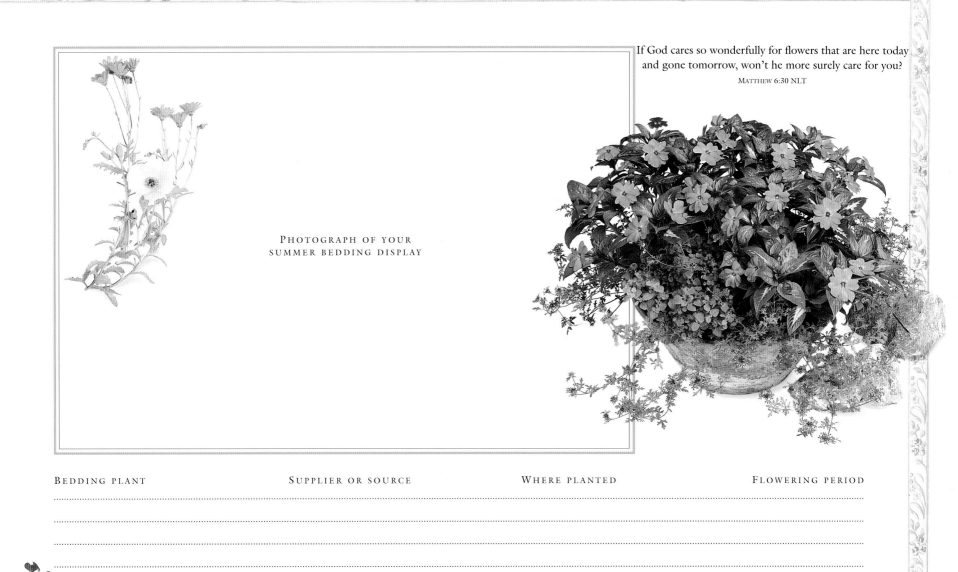

If God cares so wonderfully for flowers that are here today and gone tomorrow, won't he more surely care for you?

MATTHEW 6:30 NLT

PHOTOGRAPH OF YOUR
SUMMER BEDDING DISPLAY

BEDDING PLANT	SUPPLIER OR SOURCE	WHERE PLANTED	FLOWERING PERIOD

LATE SUMMER

TASKS TO BE DONE

CHECKLIST OF LATE SUMMER TASKS

Place plant, bulb, and seed orders with nurseries for fall delivery

Take semi-ripe and softwood cuttings of woody plants

Prune topiary, rambler roses, and most old roses

Sow seed of hardy annuals and biennials in pots for fall planting

Start cutting back shrubby herbs

SPECIAL PROJECTS

PLANTS THAT REQUIRE SPECIAL ATTENTION

IDEAS FOR FUTURE PLANTING

God the Artist
You take the brush, and the colors sing. All things have meaning and beauty in that space beyond time where you are.
DAG HAMMARSKJÖLD, *Markings*

THE GARDEN IN LATE SUMMER

PLANTS IN FLOWER

SUCCESSFUL COLOR SCHEMES

Whoever sows sparingly will also reap sparingly, and whoever sows generously will also reap generously.

2 CORINTHIANS 6:9
NIV

OUTSTANDING PLANTS

WEATHER CONDITIONS

CREATIVE COLOR

The summer palette covers the whole spectrum of color and can be as bright or as subtle as you please. Hot colors, such as reds, oranges, and yellows, look their best in the heat and brilliance of the late summer sun. Alternatively, cool colors such as pale pinks, blues, and purples can help to create a welcome feeling of respite; white flowers especially come into their own on a summer's evening, when they seem luminous in the dusk.

Color is one of the crucial elements of any planting design. Hot colors draw the eye and appear nearer, while cool colors are calming and seem more distant. Opposite colors often complement each other; for example, splashes of bold color can add sparkle to a muted color scheme, while pale hues can accentuate a fiery border. Work with related colors in differing intensities as you build confidence in your color choices.

FALL

For man, autumn is
a time of harvest, of
gathering together.
For nature, it is a
time of sowing, of
scattering abroad.

EDWIN WAY TEALE,
AUTUMN ACROSS AMERICA

Fall is a mellow time. The exuberance of summer is over, but there are still some flowers in bloom, and foliage, hips, berries, seedheads, and grasses add rich color and texture to your garden. Sunlight becomes more diffuse and gentle, and it is time for harvest. Visual emphasis moves toward the shape and color of fall foliage and bark. Some plants are at their peak, and with the herbaceous perennials mostly over, fall foliage comes into its own. The shapes and hues of plants and leaves that change color in this season can be used to great effect. Fall shades of red, orange, burgundy, and russet are rich, deep, and warm. One or two carefully placed plants with spectacularly colored leaves, offset by some later-flowering perennials in reds and yellows, will create the perfect seasonal setting for relaxation and spiritual reflection.

FALL GARDEN TASKS

Pruning
Prune deciduous trees, shrubs, and evergreen hedges.

Weeding
Control all weeds.

Mulching
Mulch established plants and borders.

Transplanting
Move established trees, shrubs, and perennials.

Dividing
Divide congested or clump-forming perennials and herbs.

Sowing
Collect and sow seeds of hardy perennials and annuals outside.

Taking cuttings
Take cuttings of tender herbaceous plants; take hardwood cuttings.

Lawns
Reseed worn areas; returf if conditions permit; aerate and apply fall fertilizer; mow and edge as necessary.

Leaves
Collect leaves as they fall, and place in a pile or mesh bin to make compost.

PHOTOGRAPH OF YOUR GARDEN
IN FALL

Planting
Plant out shrubs, climbers, hardy perennials, biennials, pot-grown trees, and spring-flowering bulbs; plant prepared bulbs in pots for forcing.

Winter protection
Pot up tender plants and bring under frost-free cover; protect the crowns of vulnerable plants in the garden; raise and winter-wrap containers.

Cutting back
Cut back dead foliage and remove stakes.

General
Clean out and disinfect the greenhouse; clean outdoor furniture and store; bring in winter-flowering plants under glass and top-dress.

EARLY FALL

TASKS TO BE DONE

CHECKLIST OF EARLY FALL TASKS

Prune evergreen hedges

Plant evergreen hedges

Take semi-ripe and leaf-bud cuttings of trees, shrubs, climbers, and herbs

Take cuttings of tender herbaceous plants

SPECIAL PROJECTS

Sing a song of seasons!
Something bright in all!
Flowers in the summer,
Fires in the fall.

ROBERT LOUIS STEVENSON,
AUTUMN FIRES

PLANTS THAT REQUIRE SPECIAL ATTENTION

IDEAS FOR FUTURE PLANTING

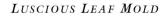

THE GARDEN IN EARLY FALL

PLANTS IN FLOWER

LUSCIOUS LEAF MOLD

Fallen leaves create an exquisite pattern of rich colors on the lawn, but they do need to be raked up and put to good use. Leaves that curl up and resist compaction, such as oak and ash, can help protect plants against frost heaving: cover the crowns of perennials that die down during the winter with a handful of leaves, and secure them with twigs. Leaves can also be left to rot down into leaf mold. Make or buy a wire mesh bin, pack the leaves in loosely, water and turn occasionally, and let them rot down. This creates a crumbly mixture that can be used as a soil conditioner or put through a sieve and added to soil mix.

OUTSTANDING PLANTS

SUCCESSFUL COLOR SCHEMES

At the proper time we will reap a harvest if we do not give up.

GALATIANS 6:9 NIV

WEATHER CONDITIONS

MID-FALL

TASKS TO BE DONE

CHECKLIST OF MID-FALL TASKS

Plant bare-root and balled-and-burlapped trees

Transplant established shrubs

Plant evergreen shrubs

Carry out layering of shrubs and climbers

Rake out thatch and aerate lawn

Take hardwood cuttings of woody plants

PLANTS THAT REQUIRE SPECIAL ATTENTION

SPECIAL PROJECTS

IDEAS FOR FUTURE PLANTING

I am the true vine,
and my Father is the gardener.
JOHN 15:1 NIV

THE GARDEN IN MID-FALL

PLANTS IN FLOWER

....

*All of the bushes
are burning now!
All of the trees
are aflame!
The woods are
alive with the
glory of God
And the leaves are
telling his name!*
ELIZABETH ROONEY,
BRIGHT LEGACY

OUTSTANDING PLANTS

....

SUCCESSFUL COLOR SCHEMES

....

SAVING SEEDS

An easy and inexpensive way of increasing your stock for next year is to collect the seeds from your favorite plants. You can also be certain that the seed is truly fresh. Many hardy annuals and perennials can be sown as soon as the seed has ripened, but it is prudent to keep some back for spring, when the seed can be used for filling in gaps between plants.

Collect the seedheads or pods in paper bags as soon as they begin to ripen or split, and let them dry out completely in a cool, airy place. If the seed is contained in a fleshy fruit or berry, soak the fruit in water to soften the fleshy coating, extract the seed and clean it, then let it dry. Separate out the seed and discard any chaff, put the seeds in labeled envelopes, and store in a cool, dark, dry place until needed.

WEATHER CONDITIONS

....

LATE FALL

TASKS TO BE DONE

CHECKLIST OF
LATE FALL TASKS

Take hardwood cuttings
of trees

Sow green manure
on bare soil

Train in new shoots
of climbers

Transplant hardy
perennials and biennials
from nursery bed to
borders

SPECIAL PROJECTS

PLANTS THAT REQUIRE SPECIAL ATTENTION

IDEAS FOR FUTURE PLANTING

The LORD will indeed give what is good,
and our land will yield its harvest.
PSALM 85:12 NIV

THE GARDEN IN LATE FALL

PLANTS IN FLOWER

OUTSTANDING PLANTS

SUCCESSFUL COLOR SCHEMES

MAKING COMPOST

Compost-making is a satisfying activity for the gardener, completing the cycle of growth and decay and providing a sumptuously fertile mixture that effectively replenishes soil nutrients. Even the smallest garden can maintain a compost pile.

Any organic matter from the kitchen and garden, laid down in layers of soft and more woody material, will rot down if the pile is kept moist and air is allowed to circulate freely. Bacteria and other organisms such as worms and insects then break up the organic matter to produce heat and the desired crumbly, sweet-smelling mixture. Turning and watering the pile occasionally speeds up decomposition. It is best not to include perennial weeds, meat and fish, or diseased prunings in a compost pile. Compost increases water retention in sandy soil and helps break up heavy clay soil.

WEATHER CONDITIONS

O God our creator,
who lives and reigns
for ever and ever.
Even the common
thornbush is aflame
with your glory.
WALTER RAUSCHENBUSCH

WINTER

The importance of good garden design is revealed in winter, when the garden is stripped down to its bones. Evergreens that provided a constant but unremarkable backdrop to more dynamic plants in the summer can be appreciated without distraction. Attune your eye to winter's subtle beauty: the delicate shapes God creates with frost on twigs, leaves, and grasses; the fragile winter sun casting elongated shadows across the lawn; the texture of bark, the color of exposed stems and bright winter berries; and the welcome sight of dainty and exquisite winter flowers. Winter is the year's rest. For maximum impact, position winter-flowering plants with perfumed flowers near the house and enjoy the fragrance from scented winter-flowering plants wafting on the crisp, clear air.

WINTER GARDEN TASKS

Pruning
Prune and renovate deciduous shrubs.

Planting
Plant out trees, shrubs, pot-grown climbers, and roses.

Transplanting
Transplant deciduous trees, young shrubs, and established roses and perennials.

Watering
Water seedlings, cuttings, bulbs, and other plants under glass if needed.

Winter protection
Make sure all plant protection remains secure; check necessary plant ties and supports are in place.

General
Service garden machinery, tools, and water pump; place orders for spring delivery with nurseries and seed companies.

PHOTOGRAPH OF YOUR GARDEN
IN WINTER

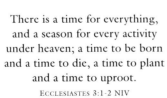

There is a time for everything, and a season for every activity under heaven; a time to be born and a time to die, a time to plant and a time to uproot.

ECCLESIASTES 3:1-2 NIV

EARLY WINTER

TASKS TO BE DONE

CHECKLIST OF EARLY WINTER TASKS

Prune and renovate deciduous trees and hedges

Take hardwood cuttings of trees, shrubs, and climbers

Finish collecting leaves

Finish clearing away plant debris and stakes

Sow seed of woody plants

PLANTS THAT REQUIRE SPECIAL ATTENTION

SPECIAL PROJECTS

IDEAS FOR FUTURE PLANTING

From all that dwell below the skies
Let the Creator's praise arise;
Let the Redeemer's name be sung
Through every land by every tongue.

ISAAC WATTS, *FROM ALL THAT DWELL BELOW THE SKIES*

THE GARDEN IN EARLY WINTER

PLANTS IN FLOWER OR IN BERRY

SUCCESSFUL COLOR SCHEMES

> *You make me glad by your deeds, O Lord; I sing for joy at the works of your hands. How great are your works, O Lord!*
>
> PSALM 92:4–5 NIV

WEATHER CONDITIONS

OUTSTANDING PLANTS

PUTTING THE GARDEN TO BED

As the days shorten and the weather becomes colder, it is time to protect the garden against the cold and winds of winter. Young, delicate plants can be protected with leaf mold, straw, or cloches and windbreaks erected as necessary. Bubble wrap can be tied around containers to be left outside, and the rest brought inside. Erect burlap screens around newly planted evergreens to protect from sun and wind. Gaps that have appeared in the mulch can be filled in, to prevent the frost from penetrating too deeply into the soil. Take advantage of the bareness of the garden and carry out general maintenance of tools, fences, and paths, or undertake structural work such as digging a pond or building a rock garden or gazebo.

Mid-and late Winter

TASKS TO BE DONE

CHECKLIST OF MID-AND LATE WINTER TASKS

Repot or top-dress trees in containers

Prepare trees for layering in spring

Prune and train hardy deciduous climbers

Graft trees and shrubs

Brush snow from shrubs and hedges

Repair storm damage

SPECIAL PROJECTS

PLANTS THAT REQUIRE SPECIAL ATTENTION

IDEAS FOR FUTURE PLANTING

This is my Father's world
and His own design.
But in His goodness
He has made it mine!

FAYE CARR ADAMS

THE GARDEN IN MID- AND LATE WINTER

PLANTS IN FLOWER OR IN BERRY

ADVANCE PLANNING

The depths of winter, when there is less to do in the garden, is an ideal time to take stock and plan for the coming year. The notes you have made during the previous seasons will prove invaluable in helping you choose which plants and seeds to buy in order to improve your garden in the following year. Now is the time to plan a whole new area and decide to try out new ideas – to incorporate plants previously unknown to you into existing planting, or to experiment with planting combinations that you have noticed and admired during the previous year.

OUTSTANDING PLANTS

SUCCESSFUL COLOR SCHEMES

Unto you, Lord God, I turn. Your print is everywhere, and everywhere divine. Where can I look and I do not see you!

WALTER WANGERIN,
*RAGMAN AND OTHER
CRIES OF FAITH*

WEATHER CONDITIONS

GARDENS VISITED

Visiting other people's gardens, whether they are well-known, or just interesting or pleasurable to look at, is a wonderful way of learning the art of gardening. You can pick up new ideas and expand the breadth of your knowledge. Seeing an unfamiliar plant growing *in situ* is an effortless way of becoming aware of new plants, and noticing a planting combination that you find particularly appealing will give you inspiration for new plants and ideas for your own garden. Making notes soon after a visit will help you remember remarkable gardens.

NAME OF GARDEN

ADDRESS

DATE OF VISIT

OUTSTANDING PLANTS

NOTES

NAME OF GARDEN

ADDRESS

DATE OF VISIT

OUTSTANDING PLANTS

NOTES

NAME OF GARDEN

ADDRESS

DATE OF VISIT

OUTSTANDING PLANTS

NOTES

NAME OF GARDEN

ADDRESS

DATE OF VISIT

OUTSTANDING PLANTS

NOTES

NAME OF GARDEN

ADDRESS

DATE OF VISIT

OUTSTANDING PLANTS

NOTES

PHOTOGRAPH OR
MEMENTO OF VISIT

NAME OF GARDEN

ADDRESS

DATE OF VISIT

OUTSTANDING PLANTS

NOTES

NAME OF GARDEN

ADDRESS

DATE OF VISIT

OUTSTANDING PLANTS

NOTES

NAME OF GARDEN

ADDRESS

DATE OF VISIT

OUTSTANDING PLANTS

NOTES

SHOWS AND LECTURES

A keen gardener is aware that there will always be a great deal to learn and many new plants and ideas to discover. Visiting horticultural shows and attending lectures or courses are enjoyable ways of augmenting your gardening knowledge. At horticultural shows you can find out about current trends in gardening and discover which new plants are being launched, while a comprehensive lecture or course can give a lot of information, and be entertaining. Use these pages to make notes of anything you wish to remember or use in your plans for the future.

HORTICULTURAL SHOWS

NAME OF SHOW

DATE OF VISIT

OUTSTANDING PLANTS

NEW PLANTS SEEN

NEW IDEAS

NEW NURSERIES AND SUPPLIERS

COMMENTS

NAME OF SHOW

DATE OF VISIT

OUTSTANDING PLANTS

NEW PLANTS SEEN

NEW IDEAS

NEW NURSERIES AND SUPPLIERS

COMMENTS

LECTURES

NAME OF SPEAKER

VENUE/DATE

TOPIC OF TALK

COMMENTS

NAME OF SHOW

DATE OF VISIT

OUTSTANDING PLANTS

NAME OF SPEAKER

VENUE/DATE

TOPIC OF TALK

COMMENTS

NEW PLANTS SEEN

NAME OF SPEAKER

VENUE/DATE

TOPIC OF TALK

NEW IDEAS

COMMENTS

NEW NURSERIES AND SUPPLIERS

NAME OF SPEAKER

VENUE/DATE

TOPIC OF TALK

COMMENTS

COMMENTS

CONTACT NAMES AND ADDRESSES

Use this section to record the details of the nurseries, suppliers, and individuals
that you use for all your gardening requirements.

NAME
....

ADDRESS
....

TELEPHONE/CONTACT NAME
....

COMMENTS
....

NAME
....

ADDRESS
....

TELEPHONE/CONTACT NAME
....

COMMENTS
....

NAME
....

ADDRESS
....

TELEPHONE
....

CONTACT NAME
....

COMMENTS
....

NAME
....

ADDRESS
....

TELEPHONE/CONTACT NAME
....

COMMENTS
....

NAME
....

ADDRESS
....

TELEPHONE/CONTACT NAME
....

COMMENTS
....

NAME
....

ADDRESS
....

TELEPHONE
....

CONTACT NAME
....

COMMENTS
....

NAME

ADDRESS

NAME

ADDRESS

TELEPHONE/CONTACT NAME

COMMENTS

TELEPHONE/CONTACT NAME

COMMENTS

NAME

ADDRESS

NAME

ADDRESS

TELEPHONE/CONTACT NAME

COMMENTS

TELEPHONE/CONTACT NAME

COMMENTS

NAME

ADDRESS

NAME

ADDRESS

TELEPHONE

CONTACT NAME

COMMENTS

TELEPHONE

CONTACT NAME

COMMENTS

MEMBERSHIP RECORDS

Use this page to record your membership details of horticultural organizations.

ORGANIZATION

MEMBERSHIP NUMBER

SUBSCRIPTION

DATE DUE

NOTES

ORGANIZATION

MEMBERSHIP NUMBER

SUBSCRIPTION

DATE DUE

NOTES

ORGANIZATION

MEMBERSHIP NUMBER

SUBSCRIPTION

DATE DUE

NOTES

ORGANIZATION

MEMBERSHIP NUMBER

SUBSCRIPTION

DATE DUE

NOTES

ACKNOWLEDGMENTS

Dorling Kindersley would like to thank the following for their
kind assistance in supplying items for special photography:
Castle Antiques, Lewes; Kennedy's Garden Centre, Hailsham;
McQueens, London.

The following photographs were reproduced by courtesy of:
Jerry Harpur, pages 4 and 60; Anne Hyde, page 34;
S. & O. Mathews, page 42.